CURRENT AFRICAN ISSUES 64

I0103454

THE NUER PASTORALISTS – BETWEEN LARGE SCALE AGRICULTURE AND VILLAGIZATION

A case study of the Lare District in the Gambella Region of Ethiopia

Wondwosen Michago Seide

THE NORDIC AFRICA INSTITUTE
UPPSALA 2017

INDEXING TERMS:

Land tenure
Pastoral economy
Pastoralists
Agricultural land
Agricultural investment
Resettlement
Villages
Ethnic groups
Nuer
Ethiopia, Gambella Region

The Nuer Pastoralists – Between Large Scale Agriculture and Villagization:
A case study of the Lare District in the Gambella Region of Ethiopia

Current African Issues (CAI) No 64

Seide, Wondwosen Michago

ISSN 0280-2171
ISBN 978-91-7106-792-0   paperback
ISBN 978-91-7106-793-7   pdf e-book
ISBN 978-91-7106-794-4   epub e-book

Cover photo: Ana Cascão, Stockholm International Water Institute (SIWI)

Layout: Henrik Alfredsson, The Nordic Africa Institute

Print on demand: Lightning Source UK Ltd.

THE NORDIC AFRICA INSTITUTE (NAI) is a centre for research, documentation
and knowledge on contemporary Africa in the Nordic region. Based in Uppsala, Sweden, the Institute is financed jointly by the governments of Sweden,
Finland and Island. The author was employed as a guest researcher with NAI
in 2014-15 and NAI has financed this publication.

CURRENT AFRICAN ISSUES (CAI) is a book series published by the Nordic Africa
Institute since 1981. As the title implies, it raises and analyses current and topical issues concerning Africa. All CAI books are academic works by researchers
in the social and multidisciplinary sciences.

The opinions expressed in this volume are those of the author and
do not necessarily reflect the views of the Nordic Africa Institute.

Print editions are available for purchase, more information can be found at
the NAI web page www.nai.uu.se.

Contents

Acknowledgments

I want to thank the Future Agricultural Consortium (FAC) for financing this research. I am particularly indebted to Dr Jeremy Lind for his critical comments and expertise, which greatly assisted the research. I appreciate the Nordic Africa Institute (NAI) for offering me a guest researcher position. I have benefited from its research environment. I would specifically like to thank Dr Terje Oestigaard at NAI for his robust academic discussion and insightful views. I also want to acknowledge the usual support of Dr Alan Nicol at the International Water Management Institute. During the fieldwork, I got considerable assistance from two research assistants and six data collectors and translators. My thanks also to two anonymous reviewers. I appreciate Semnehe Ayalew's and Lealem Mersha's comments on the manuscript. I pass my gratitude to my kind-hearted sister Meseret Michago. Finally, I want to mark my eternal affection for my mother, Alemnesh Hailgiorgis Weshmeto, who has passed away while I was in the fieldwork. I fondly dedicate this research to her – አማይዩ!

Wondwosen Michago Seide

List of maps, charts and tables

The contribution of pastoralist communities to the country's national economy has always been overlooked and underestimated

1   Introduction

1.1   Background

Ethiopia has shown encouraging economic development in the past years. The swirls of economic bubbles are impacting the different regions of the country. Unlike the past, when the borders and lowlands were largely excluded, the margins are now increasingly becoming part of the development scheme of the state. At the moment, there are several national and regional development projects being implemented in Gambella Regional State (GRS), one of Ethiopia's nine regions, or *kililochs* (Amharic language), in the west of the country, on the border with South Sudan. There is steady growth in construction and infrastructure, growing investment, a flourishing of the private sector, urbanisation, and an expanding livestock trade and exchange economy in this region. However, being part of the development scheme of the federal state does not necessarily guarantee that this peripheral region will be integrated and brought closer to the political, cultural and economic core.

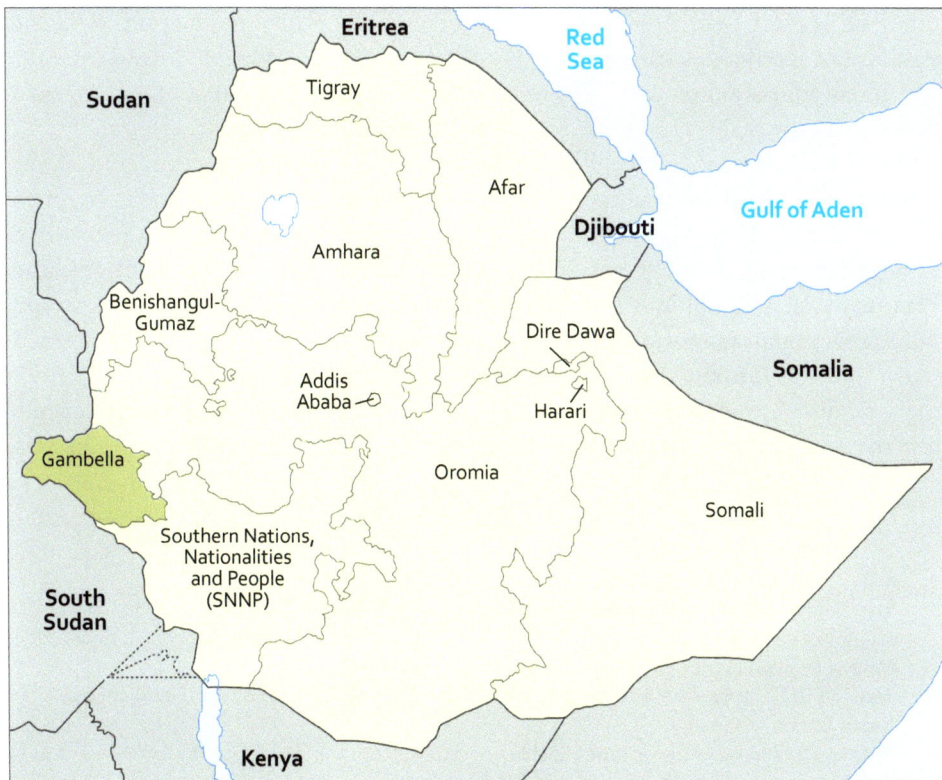

Map 1. Overall, the Federal Democratic Republic of Ethiopia is divided into nine regions, or *kililochs*, and two chartered cities (Addis Ababa and Dire Dawa).

The pastoralist way of life is one of the oldest socio-economic systems in Ethiopia. Pastoralists constitute some 29 ethnic groups and about 12 per cent of the total population.[1] The main pastoralist communities in Ethiopia are found in the regions of Afar, Somali, Oromia (Borena, Bale and Karayu zones) and Southern (Nyangatoum and Bume). Ethiopia has Africa's largest livestock population. The livestock economy covers more than 60 per cent of the country's land area in the semi-arid lowlands.[2] Nevertheless, the contribution of pastoralist communities to the country's national economy has always been overlooked and underestimated.[3] It is only recently that the government has started to give the sector the attention it deserves. Gambella is made up of large areas of agricultural and pastoral land. In Gambella, ethnic Nuer transhumant communities have always been the most marginalised groups, even among other pastoralist communities in the country. The Nuer pastoralist way of life has been troubled in many ways.

The commoditisation of land has been a significant development in the history of the modern capitalist world.[4] Land deals in Africa have been characterised by privatisation, commoditisation, enclosure, production, invention, natural reproduction and capitalisation.[5] Over 60 years ago, Karl Polanyi warned of the dangers of commoditisation of land, noting that allowing the dictates of 'market forces' determine the 'fate' of human society is tantamount to allowing the 'demolition of society'.[6] He also noted that land is more than a mere commodity or property, which has cultural value and significance specific to a community.[7] David Harvey (2003) noted that land enclosure and commoditisation of nature has resulted in the 'capital accumulation by dispossession.' This view is also supported and advanced by other authors.[8]

In recent years, the Gambella region has experienced rapid processes of land leasing. This has affected the political economy of the region and the country. The government made it clear that large-scale land investment was an important part of the country's strategy for steady development. The government's first Growth and Transformation Plan (GTP I), an ambitious five-year plan from 2010/11 to 2014/15, aimed to spur rapid agricultural transformation through the development of a large-scale commercial sector and the introduction of innovative agricultural techniques that would foster the agricultural productivity of smallholders. This plan envisaged that Ethiopia would become a food-secure, middle-income country by 2025, such that it could increase

---

1   Mohammed (2004).
2   Ibid.
3   Ibid.
4   According to Ba Gchi (2003:404), England was the first country in Western Europe to "convert land into a commodity, transferable, salable and heritable, except for restrictions which sought to preserve large properties."
5   Baker (2005); Castree (2005); Mansfield (2004); Prudham (2007); Robertson (2006) cited in Turner (2009).
6   Polanyi (1944) cited in De Schutter (2011).
7   Ibid.
8   Such as Castree (2008); Cronon (1991); Heynen et al (2007); McCarthy and Prudham (2004) cited in Turner (2009).

output of major crops from 19 to 27 million tonnes at the end of the first five-year plan.[9] To achieve this, the government has leased large tracts of land to domestic and international investors in different parts of the country, particularly in Gambella including Lare *woreda* (district).

The country's Agricultural and Rural Development Strategy clearly states that voluntary resettlement will be one of the mechanisms by which the government will try to ensure food security, bring about development, and create a conducive environment for technological transfer; and also assist the establishment of socio-economic institutions that guarantee sustained and enduring economic development, facilitate the improvement of good governance and foster the process of democratisation. The government planned to resettle 1.5 million people in the four pastoralist regions of the country: Gambella, Afar, Somali and Benishangul-Gumuz. The Gambella Regional State Villagization Programme Implementation Manual (2010), from 2010/11 to 2013/2014, had the objective of resettling the sparsely populated region settled on riversides that engaged in shifting cultivation and were exposed to natural disasters, such as floods, by moving them to safer and better settlement sites.

A noteworthy fact is that large-scale mechanised farms and villagization programmes are not new to Ethiopia or Gambella. Programmes for both ended in fiasco during the previous military regime – the Derg Regime (1974-1987) – and resulted in the exploitation of host communities especially. The same also happened in other pastoral areas. An example often cited in this regard is the case of the Awash Valley development,[10] which despite creating job opportunities for people moving to the Afar region from the highlands and providing increased food production and inputs to national industry, failed to incorporate the Afar pastoralists, who were alienated and marginalised in their own land. For example, Helland (2006) noted that 'in Afar, transformations associated with the commercial cultivation of 150,000 hectares in the Awash River basin have restricted pastoralist mobility and their use of dry and wet grazing areas'.[11]

The current government argues that resettlement and land lease would put Gambella at the centre of the state's development agenda, and would result in the improvement of people's livelihoods by creating job opportunities, establishing public services and ensuring food security at local and national levels. But this claim is not without its critics. For instance, the Oakland Institute argues that resettlement and the penetration of capital may result in the further marginalisation of the Nuer.[12] Human Rights Watch (2011) also questions the intent of the villagization programme, noting that it poses a threat to the identity and livelihoods of the Nuer pastoralists of the region.

Understanding the consequences of these state-led programmes requires rigorous sustained research and discussion. This paper is an attempt to contribute to this debate by focusing on two major themes: large-scale agriculture and the villagization pro-

9   GTP I (2010).
10   Desalgn (2009).
11   Cited in Makki (2012:8).
12   Mousseau & Sosnoff (2011), Narula et al (2013).

grammes. It examines the dynamics of Gambella's political economy and the process of incorporating the region – and the Nuer in particular – into the national economy. Specifically, it explores how processes of commercial farming investments and the villagization programme impact Nuer pastoralists. Although a growing number of studies address development in pastoral areas of Ethiopia,[13] relatively little research is being done on the Nuer. The major research questions for study are the following: how do changes in the political context and economic situation of the region affect Nuer pastoralists? How has large-scale agricultural investment affected the Nuer? How has the villagization programme affected the Nuer? How have the Nuer been affected by livelihood changes and what innovative strategy have they been employing to cope with these changes? Is there a future for Nuer pastoralists in the region? If so, what would it look like?

The contribution of this paper may be limited because the impacts of these programmes have yet to be seen. Hence, the findings of this paper indicate the potential and actual challenges of the programme, and thus are not comprehensive. This paper has five sections. The first gives the background to the study, discussing pastoralism in Gambella. The second gives an overview of the Nuer livestock trade and market. Based on the findings, the third section discusses land investment processes, their implications and the potential impact they may have on the local people. The fourth section discusses the villagization programme in relation to the developmental challenges it entails. The final section provides a conclusion and policy implications.

1.2   Methodology

This research uses primary and secondary data sources. The fieldwork was carried out in May and August 2012, with update visits in 2013, in Lare in Gambella. Primary data were collected from interviews with key informants, focus group discussions (FGDs) and a household questionnaire survey. Personal observation was also used in conducting the research. Visits were made to commercial farms, villagized *kebeles* (the lowest administrative unit) and livestock market centres. Additionally, oral histories about the region were collected during interviews with elders and community leaders. A series of semi-structured key informant interviews were conducted with policy makers, government officials at national, regional and district levels, researchers, development agents and veterinary officers; and also with agriculture, investment, economic and finance, trade and industry bureaus in Gambella and Lare. Random informal discussions and interviews with pastoralists, livestock traders and members of the local community were also conducted.

Qualitative interview data were also gathered from selected households and residents of Lare to identify impacts on livelihoods related to the government's villagi-

---

13   See Little, et al (2010a), Getachew, et. al (2004), Devereux (2007), Aklilu and Catley (2009), Yohannes, et al (2011).

zation and land investment programmes, as well as to discern challenges of conflict and drought in the region. The FGDs used a checklist of questions focusing on the villagization and land investment programmes, livelihoods challenges in the area, and trade and market activities in the region. Three FGDs were conducted with women, men and livestock traders. The livestock traders' discussion was held at the market place involving the main market actors, such as traders, buyers, trekkers and others. The women's FGD enriched the discussion by providing a gender perspective to the question of development. The FGD with men, which included elders, helped with understanding the ongoing villagization programme from the perspective of elders.

The household survey included 65 households drawn from six of the 23 *kebeles* in Lare. A questionnaire interview technique was used that included open-ended questions. The selection of households was made based on the security situation and accessibility – and on purposive sampling; in *kebeles* where villagization and commercial farming activities were undertaken, near the town of Korgan, the administrative centre of Lare.

The six *kebeles* were divided into three major purposive household groups:

- Group V: households in *kebeles* that were part of the villagization programme (37 households).
- Group B: households in *kebeles* that were part of both the government's commercial farming and villagization programmes (13 households).
- Group N: households in *kebeles* that were not part of either programme (15 households).

As mentioned above, the Nuer are a transhumant society, moving livestock from one grazing ground to another in a seasonal cycle. A preliminary visit was made in May 2012 to make a personal observation of the district and the livestock market. To be sure of finding the heads of households at their villages, data collection was made in August, during the rainy season. However, the rainy season makes villages far from Korgan inaccessible because of mud and flood. The fragile security situation meant that it was not possible to go to remote *kebeles*. In this regard, geographic coverage of households was not taken into consideration. Only those villages, which were safe and accessible from Korgan, were selected for data collection.[14]

Interviews were not recorded on tape due to the sensitivity of the issues discussed and also not to make the informants uncomfortable. A translator was used during the FGDs, household survey and in some one-to-one interviews, in cases when the interviewees did not speak Amharic. Thus, some of the information, views and perceptions may not have been adequately captured in the process of translation. Rough notes were immediately transcribed as soon as possible, to keep non-verbal communication and tone of the respondents' voices in mind. A few of the informants were interviewed more than once to clarify and crosscheck the reliability and validity of the information they provided.

---

14 It took a week to collect the data, with support from two research assistants and six data collectors.

The Nuer are the most marginalised compared to other pastoralist communities in Ethiopia

2 Nuer pastoralism: political economy and livestock marketing

This section provides an overview of Gambella and Lare, situating a discussion of Nuer pastoralism in the country's wider political economy developments. The recent trajectory of Nuer livestock-keeping follows the incorporation of Gambella into national development plans, as well as interactions between the centre and the periphery.

Map 2. Zones, woredas and rivers in Gambella Region. Based on map from Gambela Regional State Administration Bureau.

2.1   Lare woreda

Gambella is located in western Ethiopia, about 780 kilometres from the national capital Addis Ababa and covers an area of 25,294 square kilometres. It is one of the hottest regions in the country, 500 metres above sea level. The region consists of three zones – Anywaa, Nuer and Mejenger [15] – and 13 *woredas*. Lare is in the Nuer zone.[16]

According to the 2007 National Census, the population of Gambella was estimated to be 306,916 inhabitants. The region has one of the lowest population densities in Ethiopia, nine inhabitants per square kilometre. Gambella borders Oromia Regional State in the north and northeast, Southern Nations, Nationalities and Peoples Regional State in the south and South Sudan to the west. Lare is bordered to the south and east by the Anywaa zone, to the west by the Baro River, to the north by the Jikawo river and South Sudan, and to the west by Itang special woreda.[17] It has 24 kebeles, with a population of 26,068 inhabitants. The landscape consists of marshes and grasslands. The woreda enjoys an average rainfall of 1,900–2,100 millimetres. The temperature rises during summer, up to 45°C in March; and in August, during the rainy season, it reaches 27–31°C.[18] Part of Lare is also located within Gambella National Park, which occupies part of the area south of the Baro River.

The main livelihood activities of the woreda community are pastoralism and agro-pastoralism. Opportunities for petty trading, such as selling grains, stationaries and foods, have also expanded with the shift to settlement, which the influx of highlanders has also helped. The main crops that are grown in Lare are corn, maize, sweet potato, sesame and peanuts, which are produced in two farming seasons, using rain-fed and flood-receding farming schemes. An estimated 90 per cent of the land is flat and suitable for farming.[19] The Nuer keep mixed herds of cattle, sheep and goats. There are no camels in the region.

2.2   The Nuer

Five indigenous ethnic groups live in Gambella: the Anywaa, Nuer, Mejenger, Opo and Komo. These groups are distinct linguistically and in terms of the different livelihood activities they pursue. The Nuer practise transhumant pastoralism; the Anywaa and the Opo are predominantly sedentary agriculturalists; and the Mejenger combine hunting and gathering with shifting cultivation. There is also a small but growing population of

---

15   The Anywaa zone has five woredas (Gambella Zuria, Abobo, Gog, Jor and Dima), Nuer four (Lare, Jikaw, Wantaw and Akobo), and Mejenger two (Mengesh and Godere). Apart from that, there are Gambella woreda and the Itang special woreda.

16   Dereje, 2009.

17   The Itang woreda received its 'special' status in 2010 after fierce conflict between the Anywaa and Nuer over power and access to resources. Following the conflict, the Gambella administration labelled Itang as a special woreda that did not belong to either ethnic group. In this regard, the presence of several large-scale investments may bring tension between the two groups to the surface again.

18   Dereje, 2009.

19   Ibid.

migrants from the Ethiopian highlands (see Table 1). The demographic composition of the region has always been contested, because population proportion is implicated in control of political power and resource allocation. The proportion of the population identified as Nuer expanded from 40 per cent in the 1994 census to 48 in the 2007 census. Migrants have come from different parts of the country in search of jobs and also as a result of the resettlement programme of the Derg Regime, following the catastrophic famine of 1984 to 1985 that affected the country, especially the north. Highlanders comprise 13.6 per cent of the region's population[20] and are seen as distinct from the ethnic communities mentioned already. They are mainly engaged in the exchange economy and work as civil servants. The majority of the highlanders are ethnic Oromo, Amhara and Tigrean, and a variety of peoples – such as Kefocho, Kembata, Shekecho – from southern Ethiopia. There are also a significant number of South Sudanese in the region.[21]

Name of people	Population size	Regional population proportion (%)
Nuer	147,672	48.1
Anywaa	85,909	28
Mejenger	21,969	7.1
Komo	7,796	2.5
Opo	1,602	0.5
Highlander	41,968	13.6
Total	306,916	100

Table 1. Ethnic and other population groups in Gambella (CSA Census 2007).

In Ethiopia, based on the 'highland models',[22] the areas that are said to be the major pastoral areas are the regions of the Afar, Somali, Oromia (Borena, Bale and Karayu zones) and Southern (Nyangatoum and Bume). As Devereux notes 'marginalization is multi-layered.'[23] Some communities are more marginalised than other. In this regard, the Nuer are the most marginalised compared to other pastoralist communities in Ethiopia and data are lacking on the Nuer's way of life, their livestock trade and markets. The Nuer region is less institutionalised, especially compared to Borena and Afar. Non-governmental organizations (NGOs) are increasingly interested in pastoralist regions.[24] However, there has been very little NGO engagement in Gambella in general and in Nuer-inhabited woredas in particular. The Nuer are also given little attention by

---

20   It is argued that the term highlander has political significance, as it is often used to denote the central government, which has been historically represented by a 'highlander' since the late nineteenth century (Dereje, 2009).

21   According to the 2007 census, around 1,739 South Sudanese live as residents in Gambella. As early as 1960s, Gambella has been host to a considerable number of South Sudanese refugees. Occasionally, as in the 1980s, they outnumbered the locals (ibid.).

22   Mohammed (2004:6).

23   Devereux (2010:682).

24   Little et.al. (2010a).

national pastoralist forums, researchers and the state. Hence, they are underrepresented in the Pastoral Affairs Standing Committee in parliament, across ministries – for example, health and education – and even in the annual Pastoralist Day celebrated in the country. Studies by Little et al. (2010a) on 'The Retrospective Assessment of Pastoral Policies in Ethiopia, 1991–2008' and (2010b) on 'Future Scenarios for Pastoral Development in Ethiopia, 2010–2025' do not refer to the Nuer.

The Nuer pastoralists live in an area that is much greener than other pastoralist areas in the country. The feed for their livestock usually comes from open woodlands and riverine areas during rainy season and the savannah grasslands during the dry season near the Baro river. The Nuer can barely provide additional food to supplement their cattle's diet. It has been estimated that in Gambella 'of the total land area classified as natural grazing area only 64.2 per cent is currently utilised by livestock'.[25] However, in recent years, recurrent drought has shrunk pasture. Traditionally, Nuer livestock production centred on transhumant movements from wet season villages (*tot*) between June and October and dry season camps (*mai*) between November and May.[26] This practice is locally known as *ghuth*.[27] Nuer livelihoods have diversified over time. Many now practise a form of agro-pastoralism.

A Nuer village is conceived as egalitarian in structure whose purpose is to protect individual's life, property from floods and to facilitate the joint exploitation of commonly owned natural resources. Individuals are the basic units of analysis, but Nuer do not act as atomistic individuals.[28]

The Nuer have a culture of 'joint cattle herding', which is a suitable mechanism to cope with cattle raiding, theft and the threat wild animals pose. The Nuer practise joint camping, grazing, watering, fishing, arranging marriages, organising weddings and social dancing.[29] Even if cattle are collectively owned by family, and in some cases by lineage, the ownership and management of cattle rests on the head of the household. Cattle are a sign of prestige, power and assets. It is a badge of honour and economy. Hence, men have a firm grip on livestock, because whoever controls the cattle controls the family. Wives, daughters and sons have only user rights. The high importance of livestock in the lives of the Nuer life is clearly illustrated in their cattle houses, which are well built, spacious and bigger than the main houses.

Livestock house. Photo by author.

---

25 Dereje (undated).
26 Wal (1992) posits that seasonal changes also influence patterns of settlements. At the peak of the dry season, settlements are often followed by subsequent settlements, especially, between March and April. The availability of pasture invites more settlers height. Cited in Dereje (undated:7).
27 Dereje (undated).
28 Duany (1992:151-152).
29 Ibid.:152.

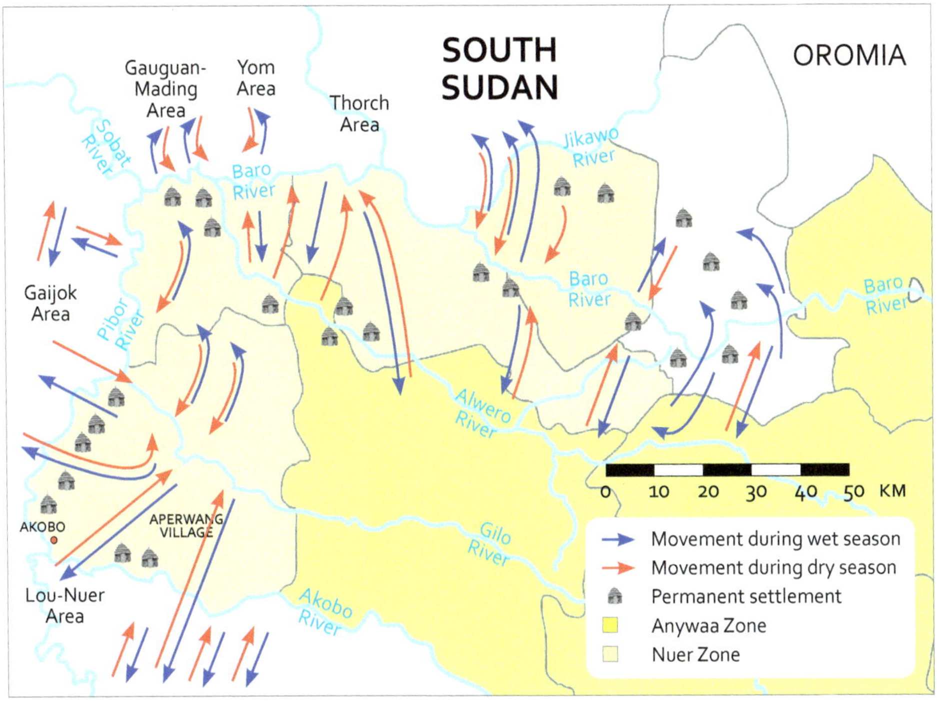

Map 3. The transhumance pattern of the Nuer. Based on Dereje (undated).

2.3 Political economy

The Gambella region was incorporated into the Ethiopian state at the end of the nineteenth century. In 1902, the international boundary between Ethiopia and Sudan was delineated between Imperial Ethiopia and the British colonial government in the Sudan after four years of diplomatic wrangling and manoeuvring.[30] During the first three decades of the twentieth century, Gambella was the economic nerve centre of the country. It served as a crucial inland port for Ethiopia's import and export trade with Sudan. Relations between the Oromo and the Nuer were based on commerce and trade. The Nuer 'traded ivory for iron and later for guns' with the Oromo and, similarly, the 'Anywaa traded cotton with the Oromo for the beads'.[31] The Nuer were engaged in cross-border trade with Sudan – present-day South Sudan – Uganda and present-day Democratic Republic of Congo.[32]

However, the Ethiopian state subjected the indigenous peoples, including the Nuer, to discrimination, alienation and slavery.[33] The establishment of the railway

30 Bahru (1976).
31 Ibid.: 11.
32 Ibid.: 63.
33 Bahru (1983); Dereje (2002).

system in the east of the country (Djibouti–Dire Dawa–Addis Ababa) monopolised Ethiopia's international trade and Gambella's significance shrunk rapidly.[34] Further, political crises in the Sudan in the 1960s and 1970s 'undermined the feasibility of the Gambella region as a trade route. Without the enclave, Gambella was gone to an economic oblivion'.[35] The significance of Gambella to Ethiopia's national development once again began to grow under the Derg Regime in the 1980s.[36] This importance can be demonstrated by the promotion in 1987 of Gambella, which came to be part of a province called Illibabore, as provincial administrative centre.[37] Following the overthrow of Mengistu's dictatorship in 1991, Gambella was given the status of a regional state in the federal structure of the country.

Conflict between the two dominant ethnic groups, the Anywaa and the Nuer, for political power has long defined the political economy of the region. The opportunistic positioning of the highlanders, who switched positions and sided with the federal government, has also played a major role in the struggle for power and resources in Gambella: "all the federal authorities in the GPNRS [Gambella People's National Regional State] are highlanders and the Anywaa and the Nuer use the same term [*Habesha*] to refer to the highlanders and the Ethiopian state. This political status of the highlanders makes them the 'significant other' in Anywaa-Nuer relations".[38]

In addition to the internal dynamics within the regional state, the geographic proximity of Gambella to South Sudan and their relations have shaped the political and economic situation of the region. The Nuer constitute the majority of the population in Gambella and are the second-largest population group in South Sudan. The Anywaa, which are the second-largest population group in Gambella, also inhabit Pochalla district in South Sudan. Relations between Ethiopia and Sudan have gone through ups and downs, from supporting each other's rebels to signing different cooperative memoranda.[39] A typical example in this regard is the effect that civil war in South Sudan has had on Gambella. Gambella has always provided refuge for those fleeing conflict in South Sudan. A quick retrospective look at the past can reveal that 'the

---

34 Bahru (1983).

35 Dereje (2002: 39).

36 The Derg Regime (1974-1987) had introduced several initiatives. For instance, it instituted a 2,500-hectare, state-owned, large-scale mechanised cotton farm in Abobo, and introduced the highly controversial resettlement and villagization programmes. The regime also carried out infrastructure development projects; for example, it constructed a dam along the Aluro river, and the Baro Bridge, and established a teacher training institute (Dereje, 2002).

37 Ibid.

38 Dereje (2002:40).

39 The government of Sudan supported the Eritrean secessionist struggle, whereas the Ethiopian government supported southern Sudanese liberation fronts. The author believes that the independent states of Eritrea and South Sudan are, to a certain extent, byproducts of the troubled relations between Ethiopia and Sudan.

Nuer and Anywaa were the pawns in the "Cold War" between Sudan and Ethiopia'.[40] The influx of refugees has resulted in a demographic impact on Gambella that has complicated ethnic relations in the region. As Dereje (2002:40) argues, 'the majority of these refugees are ethnic Nuer, thus adding to the Anywaa's demographic anxiety.'[41]

The government has a policy of creating small urban towns in rural parts of Ethiopia. The Poverty Alleviation and Sustainable Development Programme (2005/06–2009/2010) gave more emphasis to agriculture than pastoralism. Its rural and urban policies were supposed to contribute to a market-based economy.[42] The government has been investing aggressively in infrastructure to make Gambella attractive to investors. Different infrastructural activities have taken place in Lare. For instance, in March 2013 the federal government signed an agreement with Chinese and Indian companies to construct highways to connect Gambella with South Sudan, Sudan and Kenya.[43] This has brought both benefit and detriment for the people of Lare. As a result of the construction of these highways, the increasing urbanisation of the *woreda* has attracted many highlanders, who might crowd out local people.[44]

2.4   Livestock marketing

For the Nuer, cattle are a very special property and a form of social wealth. According to the FGDs, traditionally the Nuer have not been interested in selling their livestock, as the number of the cattle one owns is a source of prestige. There is less incentive to sell cattle and more incentive to accumulate. As a result, exchanging livestock for cash has not been encouraged. This has a direct impact on the livestock market in the region and beyond.[45]

2.4.1 Korgan market

The Korgan market is a domestic market that involves different villages and *kebeles* in Lare and surrounding communities. The market is held on three days each week:

---

40   For instance, waves of migrations influenced the local power balance between the Anywaa and the Nuer in Gambella. The addition of significant number of South Sudanese Nuer refugees further entrenched the numerical and political power of the Nuer, as the state, Sudan People's Liberation Army and Nuer strengthened their ties and consequently isolated the Anywaa (Medhane, 2007).

41   Dereje (2002) also makes clear that a significant number of Anywaa and Nuer diaspora communities have been created as a result of the civil war.

42   Little et al. (2010b: 26).

43   Tesfa-Alem (2013).

44   Dessalegn (2008) argues that the commercial farms generated positive 'spin-off effects' that resulted in the creation and expansion of urban centres near and around these farms. Urban centres such as Metahara, Wollechiti, Awash Station and Gewane are considered to be the offshoots of the Awash Basin Development commercial farm.

45   The livestock trade in Gambella is almost exclusively informal. The regional government does not collect systematic data on livestock. Elsewhere in Ethiopia there is very little reliable data on the livestock trade. Generally in Ethiopia, as Little et al. (2010a:12) noted, 'livestock produced and traded in pastoral areas are unreported'.

Tuesday, Thursday and Saturday. There did not used to be specific day for the livestock market, but the Lare administration decided that it should be held three days each week. The market does not have even basic facilities; watering and feeding facilities were not available at the time of visiting. Three years ago the United Nations Development Programme fenced in the market place and provided a cattle trough, but it was not working currently. According to interviewees, the market started at the same time that Korgan was established as an administrative centre ten years ago. Since then, it has expanded by leaps and bounds. In the recent past, informants noted that many South Sudanese pastoralists used to come to the market to buy cattle. This market has decreased in size since Sudan and South Sudan signed the Cooperative Peace Agreement in 2006. The relative internal peace in Sudan may have enabled South Sudanese pastoralists to focus on the internal market rather than coming to Korgan. Nonetheless, traders still come from South Sudan.

2.4.2 Gambella Town market

The Gambella Town market is open on Monday morning every week. It is organised in such a way that the other Nuer *woredas* are given access to bring their cattle and sell them. The market also accommodates Nuer *woreda* pastoralists in a rotational arrangement. Based on this arrangement, Lare has access to the Gambella Town market every three weeks. This programme was put in place by the Gambella regional administration so that all the pastoralists from each Nuer *woreda* come and trade in the market. However, pastoralists in Nuer *woredas* such as Wanthwa that are situated further away from Gambella cannot easily come to the market. Due to the proximity of Lare to Gambella Town, which is located only 75 kilometres away, villagers in Lare have been the main beneficiaries of this trade.

The Korgan market is mainly connected with the Gambella Town market. A variety of actors are involved in this market. A trekker – *chechhok* in the Nuer language – who is paid to drive cattle to the market, gets 30 Ethiopian birr (about US$ 1.75) per head of cattle.[46] The trip takes two or three days, including stops for rest. Pastoralists are also engaged in the terminal market in Itang special *woreda*, which is located between Lare and Gambella. After taking part in the Saturday morning market in Lare, the trekkers drive their cattle to Gambella. Households from villages also go directly to the Gambella Town market. Some of them pay an exit tax at the border. Informants indicated that tax collection is minimal and is carried out mainly as a formality, because most trekkers take a different route to Gambella to avoid paying.

After one-and-half days of trekking, the trekkers reach Gambella Town on Sunday in the late afternoon. The trekkers give their cattle to *yienhok*, shepherds or watchmen. Sometimes the trekkers themselves can also work as watchmen. The watchmen feed and water the cattle, and prepare them for the Monday morning market. They get 50 Ethiopian birr (about US$3) per head of cattle. A recent development is the transpor-

---

46   2012 exchange rate (1 USD = 17 ETB).

tation of goats and sheep by truck since the completion of an asphalt road between Lare and Gambella.

There are price differences between Korgan and Gambella Town livestock markets. For example, a trader could buy a fully grown ox at Korgan market for 3,500–4,000 Ethiopian birr (about US$ 210-240) and sell it at Gambella Town market for 5,000–5,500 Ethiopian birr (about US$ 300-330). The volume and price of cattle have been increased over time. The volume of livestock trade is relatively higher in those *kebeles* where there are no villagization and commercial farming activity. This is because Group N households use cattle trading as a source of income. Group N has less livelihood diversification compared to Groups V and B. Hence, Group N is the *status quo* situation. Even if these households are not in commercial farming areas, they have been affected by the presence of large commercial farms, because they block the traditional routes to the market.[47] As is discussed below in detail, the Itang special *woreda* has more than 60 domestic and international investors.[48]

Household category	Livestock production (%)	Crop production (%)	Livestock trade (%)
V	35.1	45.9	43.2
B	53	61.5	7.7
N	20.0	20.0	46.7

Table 2. Comparison of economic activities in the three household categories (Groups V, B and N).

2.4.3. Access to pasture, water and veterinary services

Most of the *kebeles* have adequate pasture and water for livestock, though the resource base shrinks each year. This is mainly related to recurrent droughts. One informant also noted that, due to perpetual fear of cattle raiding by the Murle, the Nuer do not go to remote and much greener pastures, which pushes them to use the same pasture over and again. This could explain the shrinking pasture in the villages where this research took place. The informants worried more about the Murle than commercial farming. In search of grazing land in a secure area, the Nuer are expanding into Anywaa *woredas*.[49] Historically, the Nuer have encroached on the territory of the Anywaa in Gambella and the Dinka in South Sudan,[50] which has been a cause of Nuer-Anywaa and Nuer-Dinka conflict in those areas.

---

47 Household interviews.
48 For instance, Indian investor BHO Bio Products PLC has a land leasing agreement on 27,000 hectares for 25 years (from May 2010), with the possibility of extension. This is not to say that BHO blocked the market route – this needs further research – but to indicate the size and extent of investors' presence in the area.
49 Despite the availability of expansive natural grazing land in Gambella (1,804,800 hectares), and particularly the Anywaa woreda, which constitutes 947,000 hectares of the grazing land in the region, the resource is largely underexploited because the livestock population across Abobo, Gambella, Gog and Jor is low (Dereje, 2006).
50 Bahru (1976).

Status (%)	Access to pasture			Access to water			Access to veterinary services		
	V	B	N	V	B	N	V	B	N
Getting better	48.6	38.5	33.3	59.5	30.8	53.3	27.0	23.1	20.0
Getting worse	40.5	46.2	60.0	40.5	61.5	40.0	35.1	30.8	33.3
No change	8.1	7.7	6.7	-	-	6.7	29.7	46.2	46.7
Don't know	-	7.7	-	-	-	-	8.1	-	-

Table 3. Access to pasture, water and veterinary services for animals in August 2012 compared to the same time the year before, i.e. August 2011.

For households in Groups N and B, access to water for animals worsened by 60 and 46.2 per cent respectively, while it improved by 48.6 per cent in Group V areas. In V-group, the pasture and water for animals seemed to be improving, by 59.5 and 48.6 per cent respectively, while in Group B it worsened. In Group N, access to pasture improved, while for water it worsened.

Lare has a veterinary health post and veterinary extension workers. According to the results of the household questionnaire, access to veterinary services for livestock in the Group V community was poor (27%), but better than for the Group B (23.1%) and Group N (20%) (see Table 3). It is worth noting that even if the villagized areas were improving in terms of provision of veterinary services, they generally fell behind the expected outcome of the villagization programme.

Nuer pastoralists in Gambella. Photo: Ana Cascão, Stockholm International Water Institute (SIWI)

"Whenever there is a conflict and competition between the pastoral land and farmland, land legislation by default favours agriculturalists and investors

3 Large-scale land investment

3.1 Pastoral land tenure

Land tenure is 'a central, contentious and highly flammable political theme in Ethiopia, in national as well as regional politics, in both urban and rural contexts'.[51] The land tenure system in Ethiopia has always been pro-farmer. It has overlooked or, on a few occasions, partially included pastoral land. Beruk (2003) indicates that around 1.9m hectares of rangeland had been changed to cropland.[52] In Ethiopia, since the 1960s successive governments have tried to change pastoral land into large-scale commercial farmland, as pastoral land is usually considered to be 'empty and vacant'.[53]

The 1955 Constitution of Ethiopia gave collective rights to communal land, in terms of their economic development and self-government.[54] However, it did not specifically assert pastoralist communities' right to land.[55] Rather it stated that 'all property not held and possessed in the name of any person, natural or judicial, including... all grazing lands... are State Domain'.[56] The 1975 Land Reform Proclamation dedicated four short articles to pastoral land, and granted pastoralists the 'right to grazing land.' However, at the same time it stressed that the 'primacy of government claims to land for various purpose was not in doubt'.[57]

All land in Ethiopia belongs to the state. According to Article 40 of the current Constitution of Ethiopia, which came into force in 1995, 'The Right to Property', land is common property of the nations, nationalities and peoples of Ethiopia. The constitution distinguishes between right to farmland and pastoral land:

- Article 40 (4) Ethiopian peasants have a right to obtain land without payment and the protection against eviction from their possessions. The implementation of this provision shall be specified by law.
- Article 40 (5) Ethiopian pastoralists have a right to free land for grazing and cultivation as well as the right not to be displaced from their own land. The implementation shall be specified by law.
- Article 40(6) Without prejudice to the right of Ethiopian Nations, Nationalities, and Peoples to the ownership of land, government shall ensure the right of private investors to the use of land on the basis of payment arrangements established by law. Particulars shall be determined by law.

---

51   cf. Ege (1997); Teferi Abate (2000) cited in Helland (2006).
52   Beruk (2003) cited in Flintan (2010:156).
53   Flintan (2010:156).
54   Articles 39, 43, 45–48 and 92(3).
55   Little, et al. (2010:22).
56   Helland (2006: 14).
57   Ibid.

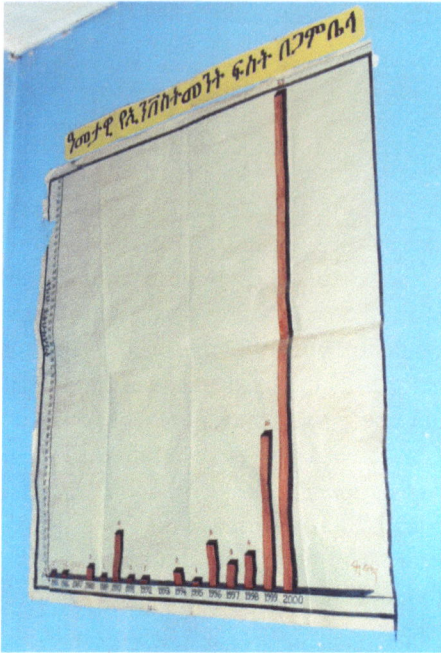

Gambella Investment Bureau. Annual investment flow in Gambella. Note: years follow the Ethiopian calendar. Photo by author.

Similarly, Article 26 of the 1975 Land Reform Proclamation stipulated that 'nomadic people shall have possessory rights over the lands they customarily use for grazing'.[58] The Federal Rural Land Administration and Utilization Proclamation 456/2005, Article 5 (3), states: 'Government being the owner of rural land can change communal rural land holdings to private holdings as may be necessary.' Even if there are legal provisions for pastoral land rights, their practical application is unclear.[59] Similarly, Mohammed (2004) argued that 'on the surface, the present legal status of pastoral land is similar to that of farmland, and the rights of pastoralists are little different from those of farmers.'[60] Devereux (2010) observed that 'Ethiopian pastoralists are incontrovertibly a 'peripheral' group in relation to the farmer-centric 'core'.[61] Whenever there is a conflict and competition between the pastoral land and farmland, land legislation by default favours agriculturalists and investors.[62]

The present author is of the opinion that the agrarian discourse in Ethiopia has mainly advocated peasant land rights. Even prominent land tenure experts have not given adequate attention to the land rights of pastoral communities. One of the main reasons for this is perhaps the impact of the 1974 social revolution, which proclaimed 'Land to the tiller' and was completely oblivious to nomadic land rights and the nomadic way of life, pastoralism. Another reason is lack of awareness and oversimplification of the pastoral sector's contribution to the national gross domestic product (GDP) and foreign exchange.[63]

Internal and external land investment-related pressures are impacting the pastoral way of life. These have brought opportunities and challenges to the Gambella region in general and to the Nuer people in Lare in particular. GTP I clearly stated that large-scale agricultural investment was at the centre of the 'government's development

58 Fouad (2012:87).
59 Little et al. (2010:22).
60 Mohammed (2004:15).
61 Devereux (2010:680).
62 Helland (2006), cited in Flintan (2010:156).
63 According to Aklilu (2002), Ethiopia's pastoral livestock sector accounted for at least 20% of the country's GDP. Hatfield and Davies (2006) also noted that Ethiopia's leather industry was also a large source of income, which generated US$41m in foreign exchange in 1998, a figure second only to the amount generated by coffee exports.

strategy'.[64] Large-scale land investment has a number of clear benefits, including promoting food security, creating jobs and transferring technology. Below is a text from an advertising poster,[65] produced by Agricultural Investment Support Directorate, Ministry of Agriculture, Ethiopia:[66]

Why invest in agriculture?
1. Boosts food security
2. Highly profitable business
3. Creates job opportunity
4. Promotes technology transfer
5. Export promotion
6. Enables capital accumulation
7. Works under and with nature
8. Environmentally-friendly business
9. Enhances land value

The main rationale that has encouraged the government's policy of commercial farming in Gambella is to increase foreign exchange earnings, create employment opportunities, facilitate technology transfer to the communities and, most importantly, to secure regional and national food security.

An informant in the Gambella regional administration office noted:

> There is ample land sufficient for all. Our region has not seen any investment activities in the past years. But now there are many investors in different sectors. Let us see the broader perspective rather than simply following a narrow approach to development.

In contrast to this statement, discussions with members of the local community indicated that investors are taking the most fertile land and less flood-prone areas near roads and rivers. Other studies support this view. For instance, Cotula (2012) noted that investors usually crave 'the best land'. In fact, personal observation during fieldwork for this study confirmed that nearly all of the land leases are located near main roads in close proximity to infrastructural facilities and transportation. Moreover, these plots are also close to the Baro river, which facilitates irrigation. Roadside agriculture can in fact be an ecological benefit in disguise, as the commercial farms do not extend into dense forest and hence they cause less deforestation.

---

64 Lavers (2011).
65 Keeley, et al. 2014, p. 12
66 Previously named the Agricultural Investment Support Directorate, under the Ministry of Agriculture (MoA), it has since been renamed and relaunched as the independent Agricultural Investment Land Administration Agency, under Council of Ministers Regulation No. 283/2013. It is believed that the newly established agency facilitates overall agricultural investment, land administration and transfer processes (MoA, 2013).

3.2 'Alienation on our turf'

Perception over land investment in the Gambella region and the Lare woreda is different. Participants in the women's FGD stated that land investment hardly brings anything to their lives. One elderly woman noted:

> I have been living in Lare *woreda* for the past three decades. In fact, I have seen changes: health posts are opening, roads have been constructed, mobile phones are now available, many shops have been opened, but I am not benefitting from any of these. So how do I expect any benefit from the large-scale commercial farms?

A man from Lare woreda echoed a similar sentiment:

> Now I see more highlanders in Lare town. There is a trend of urbanisation. But I have not received any services for my cattle. In the past, we [Nuer pastoralists] were marginalised from the economic benefit of the centre, but now we are being alienated from our *woreda*'s development. This is alienation on our turf.

Such feelings of alienation could 'erode a sense of national belonging'.[67] One informant reiterated the usual argument that the local communities were 'objects' of development when they should have been the 'subjects' and should have been properly consulted and engaged in the decision-making process.

Most community respondents did not express unequivocal opposition to land investments. Rather, they objected to being 'told what to do' while their demands seemingly fell on deaf ears, as the following quote from an elderly man from Kuerliy *kebele* shows:

> I have seen many things in life. In the past no one knew about us and came to our village. We were known to the Ethiopian government and the world through the Sudan civil war. In recent times, there are more *habeshas* [highlanders] coming to our areas. Life taught me that there are things which are inevitable. All these development activities will not be stopped whether we want it or not. They are here to share our resources. What we are asking is, if they are going to use our resources, why don't they share the benefits with us? In the Bible, there is a verse: 'rendering unto Caesar what is Caesar's and God what is God's.' Is that too much to ask?

3.3 Trekking route of the market

According to data from the Gambella Investment Bureau, nine investors – all of them domestic[68] – have taken land for farming in Lare *woreda*. It was reported that the total area of leased land is 5,400 hectares, the largest single area being 1,000 hectares, while

---

67 Coronil (2001:73).
68 A distinction is here being made between domestic investors (from elsewhere in Ethiopia; e.g 'highlanders') and indigenous investors (from Lare). See also footnote 71.

the lowest was 400 hectares. Most of this land is in the preparation phase. There are around 60 commercial agricultural farms in Itang special *woreda*, between Lare and Gambella Town.[69] During the FGDs and individual interviews it was noted that most of the respondents complained about the commercial farms in Itang, because they are increasingly blocking their trade route to Gambella Town.

The interviews and results of the household questionnaire confirmed that accessibility to the livestock market has become more difficult compared to the past (see chart 1 below). As one pastoralist informant said, 'in the past I used to go directly from my home to the Gambella town livestock market, but now I have to make another route as there are large farms in between.' This has many implications for the cattle trade. Those who are involved in trekking are now asking for more money as the route is longer than before. As discussed in previous sections, trekkers used to demand 30-40 Ethiopian birr (US$2) per head of cattle, but now the price has increased to 50-65 Ethiopian birr (US$ 3-4). Besides, the longer trade route makes the cattle skinnier and less valuable.

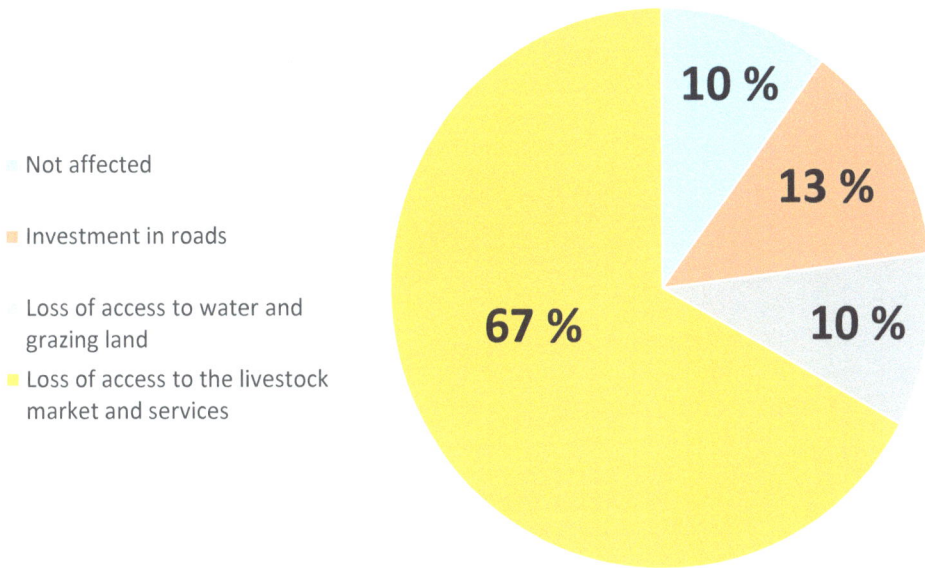

Not affected

Investment in roads

Loss of access to water and grazing land

Loss of access to the livestock market and services

10 %

13 %

10 %

67 %

Chart 1. Commercial farming and its effect on the three groups of households.

Household survey respondents were asked to draw a rough sketch of the pastoral system. It was found that the customary route has been affected, especially from Korgan to Gambella Town market. This was repeated during the FGDs. Pastoralists now take a new route to and from the two market centres; but the route from Lare to the Baro river has remained the same, as there is no commercial farm in between. The pastoralists are now following different routes, passing through and encroaching on Anywaa villages. This may affect the recently achieved fragile peace between the Anywaa and

69   There are big international farms (e.g. BHO, Karaturi) and domestic ones (e.g. Alem Farm) in the woreda.

the Nuer. Also, these new routes may expose the cattle trekkers to raids, as Itang *woreda* is commonly attacked. For instance, Dereje (2007: 79) indicated that 'on April 29, 2006, the Murle attacked [in] the Itang *woreda* seven villages of Pouldeng and looted 5,000 cattle'.

3.4 Development as a surprise

Commercial large-scale agriculture always comes as a surprise to the people of Lare. Interviews with local leaders confirmed that there is no informed or prior consent sought from communities before land is allocated to investors. One elderly person said: "It is not that we are against development, but we are against being ignored."

An official with a sectoral office in the Gambella regional office commented:

> Let alone the local people, even we are sometimes not informed about the processes. People from Addis Ababa usually decide on such important issues and simply tell us to execute their decisions without involving us in the decision making process.

An informant working in the Lare administration defended the process by noting:

> Development demands sacrifices. Sometimes, the community simply asks to be informed in advance even if they can hardly contribute to on-going activities. Passing information is a time consuming processes and we do not have time to inform everybody.

Decisions concerning land leases are highly centralised and opaque. Even senior *woreda* officials in Lare were unaware of the number of investors within the *woreda*. However, the Gambella regional administration official countered that:

> We should not be surprised that the Lare *woreda* administrators do not know the number of investors, this is mainly due to lack of communication and information exchange and has nothing to do with transparency.

Still, one can hardly expect the local community to know about investors if *woreda* administrators themselves are not fully aware of the land-leasing process. However, when we come to the villagization programme, communities are well informed in advance about the programme through different meetings with the *kebele* and *woreda* administrations.

Agricultural laborers working for the Saudi Star project in Gambella.

3.5 Types of investors

As has been discussed above, recent land investment in Lare and surrounding *woredas* has created problems concerning the route to market, as well as access to grazing land and water points. However, considering the trend of the influx of capital into the region, this situation may change in the near future. Most of the investors have not yet started full production. They are in the preparation phase. So it would be difficult to assess the contribution of these large-scale farms to employment among the Lare *woreda* community. Thus, the contribution of land investment to food security at local, regional and national levels has yet to be seen.

Few indigenous investors

The field visit and various interviews show that there are no indigenous investors in Lare,[70] even if there are many among the Nuer and Anywaa diaspora communities living

---

70   Regarding the distinction between domestic and indigenous investors, see footnote 68.

in the US and Australia.[71] Highlanders have dominated most, if not all, of the investment sector and continue to do so. 'Out of the 142 investors registered by the end of 2008 only 2 were from the indigenous people. The rest are people who are classified as Highlanders'.[72] A combination of cultural factors have disadvantaged the Anywaa, the Nuer and the Mejenger in their participation in the business sector. This is widening the economic gap between highlanders and indigenous people.[73] The sheer absence of indigenous investors may create a sense of being exploited among the local community.

Ghost investors, pseudo-investors and speculative investors

In Ethiopia, there is no requirement that obliges investors to cater for the local market and needs.[74] The few contracts reviewed, for investors such as Saudi Star and BHO Bio PLC, showed that it is up to land lessees to decide where to sell their products. According to an informant from the Itang Agricultural Bureau, 'there are investors of whom we have lost track. Their phones are not working. They are not paying their annual fees. As a result, we have revoked their licences.' We might refer to these as 'ghost investors'. Others are engaged in illegal businesses such as timber production and trade. There are also 'pseudo investors',[75] who are using their land investment licenses to secure/underwrite mortgages to borrow money from the bank. Investors who are not interested in commercial farming activities also buy land. These are what White *et al.* (2012) called 'speculative investors'.[76]

Investors using ox-drawn ploughs

Some investors do not even have the capacity to use the land properly. As one respondent mockingly noted, 'we were told that the investors would introduce efficient farming technology to our locality, instead they are using ox-drawn plough to till the land just like us'. What is happening now in Gambella was in fact observed during the

---

71 The regional government has tried to encourage the diaspora community to invest in Gambella. However, it was proved unsuccessful as the latter set a political pre-condition. On 13 December 2003, the Anywaa diaspora community made an official request to the Ethiopian government to formally apologise for siding with highlanders who had fought the Anywaa (Dereje, 2009).

72 Dereje (2009:15).

73 Ibid.

74 Countries vary in their approach to land lease contracts. Sudan, for instance, gives investors the freedom to sell abroad or locally. The preamble of the Mali-1 deal identifies food security and self-sufficiency as objectives; its main text, however, offers no rules on product marketing. In Liberia, investors may export rice only if local needs are met .In Madagascar, the law provides quotas for rice, wheat and maize, except where 'situation or circumstances otherwise demanded' (Cotula, L., 2011: 37).

75 In the report on the Humera farming project, such investors were labelled 'transient farmers'; they are not farmers by profession and do not reside on their farms (Dessalegn, 2008:103).

76 Following the international financial crisis in late 2009, investors were interested in tangible assets such as farmland. Some private equity groups have already established 'farmland funds' (Hall, 2011).

previous regime. As Dessalegn (2008) noted, the landlords evicted peasants not only for mechanised cultivation, but also to use ox-drawn ploughs to cultivate the land.[77]

3.6   Employment

According to data from Gambella Investment Bureau in December 2012, there were 332 investors (276 in agriculture, 11 in industry and 45 in services).[78] There were 77,535 employment opportunities (11,133 permanent and 66,402 temporary).[79] Investment created an influx of highlanders. In Lare there are only very few job opportunities for the local people as a result of land investment. As a respondent in Lare noted, 'there are two farms between Lare and South Sudan, but we see more highlanders than Nuer working there.'[80] Highlanders,[81] or 'ethnic strangers' as Mahmoud (2003) called them, usually take jobs. In Lare, one can easily see that highlanders own most small businesses such as petty trading activities, shops, restaurants and stationers. Only a few Nuer people have the chance to work on commercial farms, as daily labourers, tea providers and messengers. The author saw some of the local daily labourers during a visit to the Indian BHO farm in Itang, next to Lare. Pastoralists often lack the education and skills to get salaried positions on farms. Indeed, this is also the case in Afar, Borena and other pastoralist regions in Ethiopia.

The exception to this general trend is the Somali region, where the Somali people own many of the business activities in their localities.[82] In the Awash valley, the Afar pastoralists have little opportunity to participate in commercial investment activities taking place in their region. Migrant labourers from neighbouring regions have taken most of the job opportunities that the commercial farms provide, for instance at Setit Humera. This has resulted in the marginalisation of Afar pastoralists in their own land.[83] This may be repeated in Gambella, unless the federal government and Gambella

---

77   'The third five year plan encouraged commercial mechanized farming while the fourth five year plan discouraged commercial mechanized farms mainly because of the failure of commercial farming in producing the desired outcome in the previous five year plan'; report of the planning commission of 1973, also cited in Dessalegn (2008:97).

78   Telephone conversation.

79   Saudi Star, which has a 10,000-hectare lease in Gambella, claims that at present the company employs 2,000 people, with 500 permanent staff and 1,500 semi-permanent staff. When the 10,000 hectares are fully operational Saudi Star expects that 7,500 people will be employed (excluding processing) (Keely et al., 2013: 38).

80   Unlike in the past, there are currently four flights per week and a regular bus to Gambella. Increasing numbers of highlanders travel there for various opportunities.

81   This has always been a concern, even before the introduction of the land investment programme. For instance, in 2005 the Gambella Peoples' Liberation Movement/Force, a guerrilla liberation group, demanded that the government 'stop settlement of Highlanders in the region'. The group argued that the highlanders settled with the intention of making locals minorities and controlling regional politics and resources (Sommer, 2005).

82   Mussa (2004).

83   Dessalegn (2009:82–100).

regional administration try to regulate in-country economic migrants who are now monopolising the job market.

Meagre employment returns

During the FGDs, one person noted:

> I have ten cattle and twenty shoats [at the time of the field work], this is roughly equivalent to 80,000 Ethiopian Birr], but on the farm they pay me 350 Ethiopian birr per month [4,200 Ethiopian Birr per annum] as a security guard. My annual salary is less than the price of an ox.

For members of the community the rational economic choice is not to be employed on the farm. Observations made in the field in this research show that most of the employees on commercial farms are either young academically educated people, who are not involved in pastoralist activities, or people who are very poor with no or little access to resources. As an elderly man in Lare woreda noted:

> The *woreda* administration is telling us that commercial farming in our area would provide job opportunities for us. But what they do not inform us is what it does to our livestock.

As it stands, there is no investment in livestock resource available, even if there is immense potential in animal agriculture. Instead the focus of investment farming has been on land not on livestock.

Forage development

In Gambella there was 'no other food' for livestock except the natural grasses.[84] As explained above, livestock use open woodland and riverine forest during wet season and the savannah grasslands during dry season. Hence, there is a dire need for supplementary food. A 2009 report on the agricultural potential of Ethiopia by the Ministry of Agriculture (MoA), formally known as the Ministry of Agriculture and Rural Development (MOARD), stated, 'there is a potential for investment in fodder production.'[85]

the First Growth and Transformation Plan (GTP-I) also stated that it will focus on livestock development; water for people and livestock; forage development.[86] Despite its potential and government plans, the livestock sector has not been adequately exploited. The main types of crops are cash crops, cereals and in-demand plants such

---

84   Dereje (2006)
85   MOARD (2009:18) contains a more detailed summary of livestock investment potential area by region, zone and a number of woredas. The other type of animal feed that has not been developed yet and that could be produced for domestic and export market is bagged hay.
86   Five-Year Growth and Transformation Plan (FYGTP) for 2010/11-2014/15, p. 22-24.

as jatropha and sesame. An introduction of 'forage crop cultivation' for cattle would address the main problem that pastoralists face: shortage of feed.[87] According to informants, in Lare and its surroundings there is not a single investor in this sector. A domestic investor indicated that 'there is no incentive for us to invest in the livestock sector'.

Crop residue

Another source of animal feed could be crop residue from large-scale commercial farming. An animal health respondent who was questioned in relation to alternative feed for animals noted that if the investors could sell crop residue to the local community at low cost this would improve relations between investors and pastoralists. In fact, this would be a good opportunity to benefit the Nuer without changing their way of life. Instead of simply attempting to employ the Nuer on farms, selling crop residue to the Nuer to feed their livestock could foster a symbiotic relationship between land investment and pastoral activity. The global debate on land has long focused on the questions of how much commercial farming contributes to local and national food security and how much it contributes in terms of foreign exchange earnings and employment opportunities in a country. However, the present author is of the opinion that in Lare the question of how much commercial farms contribute to livestock development also needs to be included.

---

87 Currently, as Mosley (2012) noted, the export of hay and other by-products to neighbouring countries, especially Djibouti, is creating a shortage of feed in the country.

Although it would be reductionist to describe pastoralism just in terms of mobility, pastoralism is inherently a mobile way of life

4   Villagization

Villagization is not a new phenomenon. The first villagization/resettlement program-me took place in the 1980s during the Derg Regime. Gambella received settlers from the highlands, specifically from Wolo in the north and Kembata in the south. The pro-gramme was mainly carried out without the consent either of the people being resettled or host communities. Thus, it was doomed to fail.[88] Since then, the communities that were subjected to these involuntary resettlement and villagization programmes have reacted in various ways. While some accepted them, others resisted by non-compliance and yet others rejected them vehemently. A minority participated in the programmes voluntarily, anticipating that they would accrue certain benefits.[89]

The Gambella Regional State's Villagization Programme Implementation Manual (July 2010) states that 'villagization is a voluntary, study-based and water (basin)-based program.'[90] The programme planned over three consecutive years (2010/11–2012/13) to villagize 45,000 households to ensure food security, provide infrastructure and ul-timately bring sound economic development to the villagized community. Implemen-tation of the villagization programme in Lare began in 2010 in four centres: Kermchar, Kuley, Konwal and Iteya. The objective of the programme was to relocate the pastora-list community settled on riversides, where they were exposed to natural disasters such as floods, to ensure food security, accessibility to development and good governance and gain equal benefit and growth.

The programme identifies three zones as possible sites for resettlement – the Nuer, Anywaa and Mejenger – and will, among other things, provide the following:[91]

- The regional administration will provide three to four hectares of land to each household to enable the settlers to harvest within a short time, depending on the fertility of the area. However, changes may be made in the future in line with the number of families and settlers to be included in the programme during the coming years.

- The government will provide public services such as water points, health posts, education and roads (major and connecting).

- The government will provide a monthly food ration during the movement of the settlers from their origin until the next harvest season (for at least 8 months).

- Attention will also be given to ensuring the peace and security of the settlers in their new villages.

---

88 Rahmeto (2009).
89 Ibid.
90 Gambella Regional State (2010).
91 Ibid.

Pastoralists and farmers – different impacts

Villagization has different impacts on pastoralists and farmers. For agriculturalists, villagization is a relocation process. For pastoralists, however, it is a change to their way of life and mode of production that alters the basic ways in which they relate with their natural environment, and thus brings about radical changes in their social and cultural organisation. Villagization programmes inherently restrict mobility. The 'discourses of civilization' favour a sedentary life.[92] This goes with what Van der Post (1987: 79) called the 'static absolute', a discourse rooted in sedentary life as a basis of sustainable and enduring development. Policies of urbanisation, commercialisation, agricultural intensification, livelihood diversification, industrialisation, liberalisation, decentralisation and regionalisation and the like require and even assume a sedentary society.[93] On the other hand, mobility is not only a strategy of survival and livelihood; it is also a marker and manifestation of people's identity as pastoralists. But associating mobility with identity can sometimes be problematic, especially when pastoralists start a sedentary way of life, as ex-pastoralists preserve certain aspects of their former identity as pastoralists. Therefore, although it would be reductionist to describe pastoralism just in terms of mobility, pastoralism is inherently a mobile way of life.

The major discursive difference between the government and the pastoralists regarding mobility is reflected in the villagization programme. Rettberg (2010: 270) in her work on Afar pastoralists, noted that the 'state's discursive risk construction of "pastoral backwardness" in cultural and economic terms legitimises authoritarian interventions that intend to transform mobile pastoralists into sedentarised and urbanised agro-pastoralists and wage-labourers.' Devereux (2010: 691) in his research on the Somali pastoralists presented the sentiment of pastoral communities about a sedentary way of life as follows: 'Why are the farmers always telling us (pastoralists) to become farmers like them? We never tell them to become pastoralists like us.'

The perspective of the government

From the perspective of the government, a sedentary way of life is regarded as a path to modernisation and development. Pastoralists are seen as incompatible with the country's development plan. A government official in Gambella stated:

> These people do not listen, *weha keda weha melese newe*, [it's like pouring water into a bottomless bucket]… we settle them in a village and the next day they go back to their previous place… they do not listen… it is better to let them live chasing the tail of their cattle.

Such attitudes are not the official position of the government, but some people who are involved in implementing the programme hold such attitudes towards pastoralism and pastoralists.

---

92   Coronil (2001).
93   McDowell and de Haan (1997).

The villagization manual noted that villagization and land investment 'work to-gether' for the development of the Gambella region. The manual clearly states that 'villagization should be supportive [of land] investment'.[94] In contrast, the Oakland Institute argues that 'the large-scale program of villagization currently unfolding in these regions is proving serviceable to the land grabs'.[95] Fieldwork uncovered little evidence of a direct causal link between villagization and land investment, backing up the findings of another recent study by Keely *et al.* (2013).

The 'highlanderised' policymaking

The Ministry of Federal Affairs (MoFA) has been responsible for the policy formulation and implementation of villagization, with little room for participation by professionals from other ministries and federal offices such as the Ministry of Agriculture (MoA) and the Investment Agency. This may lead to a monopoly on and securitisation of the development and investment policy by MoFA and the federal government.[96] According to an informant from the Gambella regional administration, 'the policy making process is highly centralised' and 'highlanderised.' In fact, since 'the start of commercial farming, the Gambella regional government's power has been dwindling by the day.' The permanent presence of MoFA staff at the Gambella regional administration's offices, with a room next to the regional president's office, attests to this view. People in Gambella perceive the daily involvement of MoFA staff in the internal affairs of the region as encroaching on their regional constitutional autonomy and compromising their real power in the internal affairs of their region.

Ghost households

Interviews and FGDs have revealed the existence of what might be called 'ghost households' in the villagized areas. In the village visited for this study, huts have been deserted by their supposed occupants. The huts have been built shabbily to avoid any spat with the village administration. This shows how the villagers are subtly resisting the government plan. Currently, according to informants, there are only a few ghost households. However, unless the regional administration has a serious consultation with the community about why many households are not willing to resettle in the new villages, the increasing number of ghost households could lead to 'ghost villages.'

Sources of conflict and constraint

The villagization programme distributes hand tools and household items among the community. However, as an informant from the villagization office in the regional administration stated, the bureaucratic procurement process of buying these materials

---

94   Gambella Regional State (2010:8)
95   Mousseau & Sosnoff (2011:38), cited in Makki (2012:98).
96   Little et al. (2010b).

has made the implementation process very slow. He added that 'we are buying the materials from Addis Ababa and this takes a lot of time. And this is one of the reasons for the delay of implementation.'

The main livelihood challenges respondents to the household survey identified include the recurrence of drought, floods, livestock diseases, cattle raiding, loss of grazing land, villagization and establishment of commercial farms in their surroundings. It was determined that drought is still recurrent in the three categories that the research identified. But drought has less impact Group N. This is mainly because Group N households are less prone to drought due to their mobile way of life, which enables them to circumvent the adverse effects of being fixed to a locality.

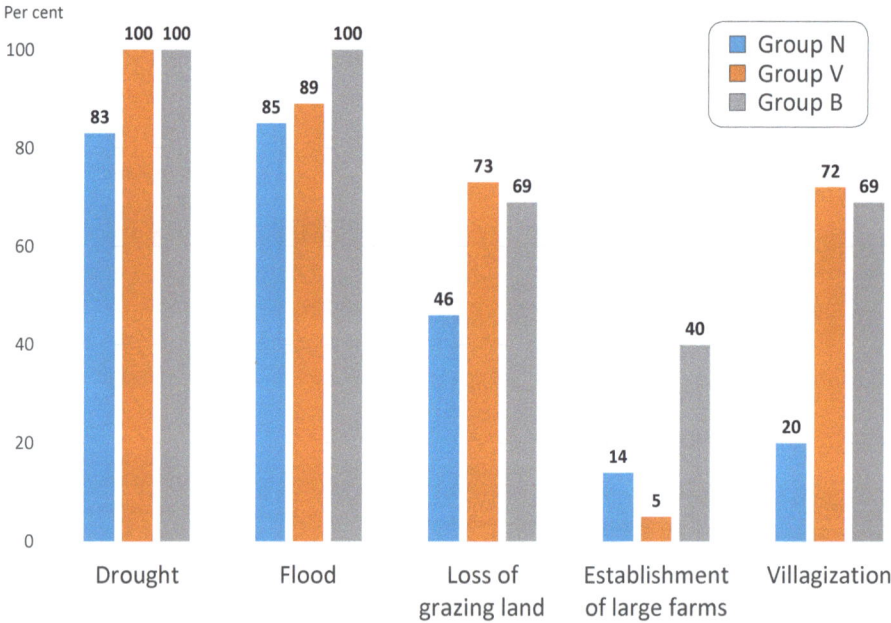

Chart 2. Proportion of households reporting livelihood challenges in Lare *woreda*.

In Groups V and B people see the villagization and commercial farm programmes as serious challenges to their livelihood. As can be seen in Chart 2 above, more than 70 per cent of Group V and Group B households consider the villagization programme as much a livelihood challenge as droughts and floods. Droughts and floods are considered a serious challenge in all the three household groups. Some 40 per cent of the Group B households consider the establishment of commercial farms to be potential threat to their livelihood. On the other hand, in Group N households only 15 and 20 per cent, respectively, see commercial farming and villagization as major threats to their livelihood. Based on the household data, FGDs and key informant interviews, Lare *woreda* residents consider villagization and commercial farming as emerging challenges to their way of life and security.

However, commercial farming activities and villagization do not seem to be major sources of conflict and constraint in the region. Respondents identified drought as the main driver of conflict. In Group V, 95 per cent of households reported that drought was one of the main causes of conflict in their localities; in Group B, 82 per cent; and in Group N, 92 per cent, as the graphs below show.

Per cent

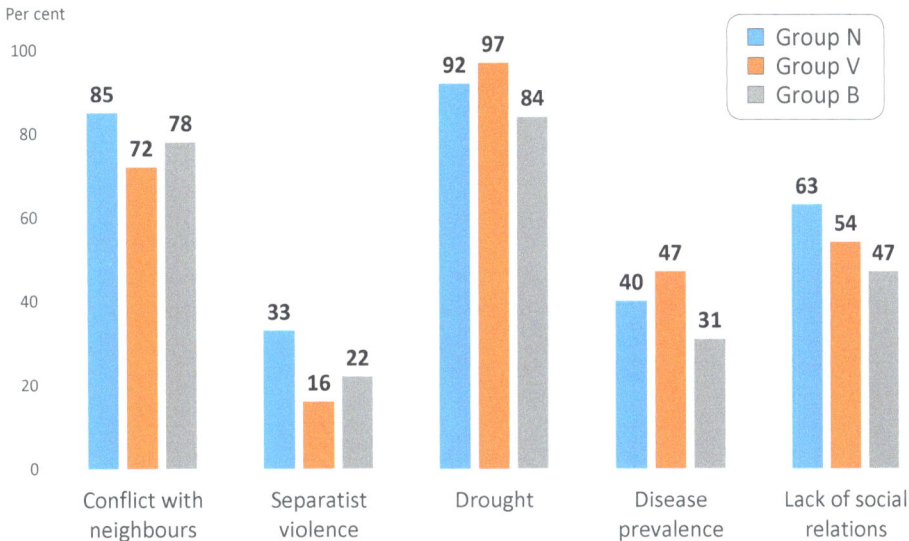

Chart 3. Proportion of households reporting sources of conflict and constraints in Lare *woreda*.

Cattle raiding

Another factor that affects the villagization programme in Lare is cattle raiding. While those resettled escape food insecurity, through receiving food rations, their resettlement may expose them to this risk factor. For the Nuer, Murle is synonymous with cattle raiding. The Murle cattle raids are among the major livelihood challenges and sources of insecurity in the area. They represent the sum of all fears and insecurities. Hence, the government has to protect the villagers from the Murle or settle them in an area far from cattle rustling. An informant in the Lare *woreda* administration said that it was forming 'three community militias' per *kebele* to avoid the cattle rustling. One respondent noted: "I used to own 30 cattle. The Murle took all my cattle and now I am engaged in daily labour work". Another informant noted: "You can run away from [the] commercial farm, subtly avoid villagization, but you cannot escape the Murle. They are raiding our livestock to our doorsteps".

Similarly, an elderly informant noted: "In the past, the raid was mainly near the Baro river bank and other remote areas. And the raids occurred during the night times, but nowadays, it is happening at our backyards, in open day light".

During the FGDs, community members frequently stated that cattle raiding was affecting livestock productivity and creating problems in terms of the safety of the livestock trade routes in the region. According to informants, the Murle had been trying to steal cattle from trekkers when they were on the way from Lare to Gambella Town. The frequency of these cattle raids had reached an alarming rate.[97]

The Murle's raids have taken a different shape as they are now strategically basing themselves in the Nuer *woreda*, and they use sophisticated weaponry and forge strategic alliances with other ethnic groups such as the Bume and Nyangatoum from southern Ethiopia. [98]

Factors affecting villagization

One respondent from Group V said:

> Personally, I have no objection to the villagization program, but it seems that it does not get the essence of our life. As you can see, the bigger cottage is for our livestock, while the smaller one is for us. This can tell you how much we value our livestock. But in the new villages there are no veterinary services. There is a risk of getting cattle diseases in the areas where we are resettled.

Another respondent added that, the villagization programme does not provide housing for the pastoralists. And this is complicated by the high cost of constructing houses. Thus, pastoralists sometimes avoid new villages, unable or unwilling to incur these additional costs. Community perceptions of the villagization programme also vary according to gender and generational factors. In an FGD, one elder commented:

> Accepting the villagization program is not simply a matter of the government promising to provide social services, it is also about staying in the same village where our memories are lived and buried. To be frank, let alone to go to another village, I am not even willing to change my chair's position, from where I sit and gaze at the sunset. I am very old. I like what I had and have, rather than what I will have.

However, younger members of the community seem to be willing to relocate to another area as long as the promised social services are provided. Sontag aptly observed 'use of 'place' as an emotional site'.[99] Old people attach themselves to their villages, as a landscape has 'layers of history'.[100] Landscape is 'a living link between what we were and what we have become... Landscape and identity are inherent components of our culture, one informing the other... spiritual and symbolic meanings people ascribe to

---

97 Dereje (2007: 79-80) gives examples of how Murle cattle raiders on a number of occasions have attacked, killed and wounded people and looted cattle in Nuer villages in Lare and elsewhere.
98 The Nyangatom and the Bume in Southern Ethiopia form part of wider Murle society and have a cross-border settlement (ibid.).
99 Susan Sontag, cited in Meyer (2007).
100 Meinig (1979:43), cited in Gerike (n.d.).

their landscape'.[101] After all, as scholars such as Baxter have noted 'pastoralism is not only a mode of production, but also a "mode of perception"',[102] as it occurs 'under a variety of social and historical conditions'.[103] This study also shows that attachment to one's landscape is one of the reasons why some rejected the villagization programme and chose not to be villagized.

Findings of fieldwork carried out in Lare show that women are more receptive to villagization than are men. A widow in the women's FGDs stated:

> I was willing to take part in the villagization program, but my husband scolded me. Now he is dead, therefore, I am free to go to the new village. My children will benefit from school. And I will get relief from grinding corn by myself as the programme would provide a grinding mill that women use commonly.

Participants in the same women's FGD were resoundingly supportive of villagization because of the perceived improvement in access to public services such as school, for their children; the construction of water points, which reduce the time women spend in their daily labour routines fetching water, sometimes from far away; and a grinding mill, which saves them pain and energy spent grinding corn manually, which causes back pain and swollen palms. A representative from the regional bureau for women and children's affairs[104] also supported this view, saying that women's perception of the villagization programme was significantly different from men's. Elsewhere, Devereux (2007:24) has noted that 'Somali women see pastoralism not as "Somali culture", but as "men's culture", and they can see many advantages to move from the "margins" closer to the "centre."'[105] Similarly, Nuer women see the villagization programme as a move towards urbanisation and access to public utilities.

---

101 Taylor (2008:7).

102 Baxter, P.T.W., & Hogg, R. (1990). Markakis (2004:14), cited in Hagmann and Speranza (2010).

103 Samatar (1992:105), cited in Hagmann and Speranza (2010).

104 The Women's and Children's Affairs Bureau and the Head of the Youth and Sport Bureau are members of the Steering Committee of the Villagization Programme (Gambella Regional State, 2010).

105 Devereux (2007:24).

The federal government and Gambella regional administration need to regulate in-country job migrants who appear to be monopolising the job market

5   Conclusions and policy implications

Almost four decades ago, the future of pastoralism was discussed at the Future of Pastoral Peoples Conference.[106] Unfortunately, the future of pastoralism has not yet been clearly charted out. Rather, its future is now being challenged by the new wave of large-scale agricultural investment and villagization programmes, which have been defining the landscape of Gambella in general and Lare in particular. This, in turn, has brought the problem of the Nuer pastoralists to the attention of the public. Whether these schemes consider the Nuer community as a subject/agent or an object of development remains debatable.

Current activities in Lare are geared more towards developing pastoral areas than protecting – much less encouraging – Nuer pastoralism as a way of life. In fact, all previous and existing development policies and strategies have discouraged mobile herders and promoted a sedentary way of life. The government's position, as stated in its Pastoral Development Policy, is to develop the pastoral regions, rather than maintaining pastoralism. According to Little *et al.* (2008: 595) this kind of approach reinforces the age-old 'impulses to transform pastoralism through outside intervention "for their own good", a paternalistic treatment of "noble savages"'.[107] They further note: 'what is not needed is another development label (stereotype) that equates pastoralism with poverty, thereby empowering outside interests to transform rather than strengthen pastoral livelihoods.' This view is also supported by ecology scholars.[108] In contrast, scholars such as Sandford recommend a pastoral area development strategy and insist on 'a future outside of pastoralism'.[109] The present author, however, is of the opinion that there should be a policy that acknowledges the nexus between two pastoral development approaches – pastoral area development vs. pastoralism development – so as to make them run in tandem without one excluding the other. Rather, they could be mutually reinforcing. This way pastoralism could be promoted while resources are developed.

The major difference between the government and pastoralists regarding mobility is reflected in the villagization programme. This study has tried to show different members of households and community in Lare perceive villagization differently. Responses to the villagization programme are not homogeneous. Community perceptions of the villagization programme vary according to gender and generational dynamics. The application of the intra-household approach is crucial to understanding the community response towards the villagization programme. Attachment to one's land is one of the reasons why some rejected the programme and chose not to be villagized.

This is not to say that the political, social and economic drivers of villagization are not relevant in determining the community response. Rather, what this research reveals

---

106 Moritz (2008).
107 Little et al. (2008: 595).
108 Such as Ellis and Swift (1988), Behnke et al. (1993), Scoones (1995), Warren (1995), cited in Hagmann and Speranza (2010).
109 Sandford (2006:4), cited in Hagmann and Speranza (2010).

is that there are often 'forgotten dimensions' that need to be taken seriously to have a nuanced understanding of the villagization programme in Gambella. Additionally, it was found that the 'degrading attitude' of the villagization programme's implementers towards the local community, might compromise successful implementation of the programme. Hence, policy-related research needs to probe to what extent the condescending attitude of highlanders is compromising the implementation process.

The other major question in this study was how much commercial farms contributed to livestock development. It has been indicated that 'a symbiotic relationship' between investors and pastoralists, and also between investors and livestock, may lead to a win-win development solution. The present author holds that revisiting the conventional question 'What is the contribution of land investment to food security, employment and for GDP?' is necessary. This question should be asked together with other relevant questions when it comes pastoral areas. These include to what extent land investment contributes to livestock production.

In Lare, livestock investment is completely absent. Expanding drought has shrunk the size of open woodland and savannah. Hence, the private sector's participation in the production of animal feeds is very necessary. The government, therefore, needs to provide incentives for investors to invest in animal resources and forage crop cultivation. The production of crops that can be used as animal fodder could be a good starting point to synchronise investment with local livestock production that could work towards creating a symbiotic relationship between investors and Nuer pastoralists.

This study found that land leasing is a highly centralised and confidential process with limited consultation of the pastoralists. However, pastoral communities are informed in advance of upcoming villagization programmes. It also found that there is insufficient evidence to show a direct causal link between villagization and land investment. The research further indicated that commercial farms are blocking traditional market routes. The author is of the opinion that policymakers could emulate Mali's pastoral trade policy. The government of Mali by law recognises livestock mobility routes to market, pasture and water.[110] Policymakers, therefore, need to respect and sanction traditional cattle routes between Lare and Gambella Town market. This could avoid potential conflicts between pastoralists and commercial land investors.

The land investment boom in the Gambella region and Lare *woreda* has created an influx of highlanders. Highlanders usually take available jobs, because the pastoralists often lack the education and skills to get salaried positions on commercial farms. Dissatisfaction is growing among the Nuer that the highlanders have stolen the limited job opportunities in the region. This may pose a serious challenge to the fragile relationship between 'indigenous people' and 'ethnic strangers'. As Dereje (2006) has observed, 'in the context of Gambella, investment has always resulted in the growing economic dominance of the highlanders.' The federal government and Gambella regional administration therefore need to regulate in-country job migrants who appear to be monopolising the job market.

---

110 Little et al. (2010b).

Bibliography

Aklilu, Y. (2002). *An Audit of the Livestock Marketing Status in Kenya, Ethiopia and Sudan.* OAU/Inter African Bureau for Animal Resources, I and II.

Aklilu Y. and Catley A. (2009). *Livestock Exports from the Horn of Africa: An Analysis of Benefits by Pastoralist Wealth Group and Policy Implications.* Feinstein International Center, Tufts University.

Ba Gchi, A. K. (2003). *The Developmental State in History and in the Twentieth Century,* Lectures delivered under the auspices of North Eastern Regional Centre of the ICSSR and the North Eastern Hill University, Shillong, 12-13 March 2003.

Bahru, Z. (1976). *Relations between Ethiopia and the Sudan on the Western Ethiopian Frontier, 1898 to 1935.* PhD Dissertation, University of London.

Bahru, Z. (1987). *An overview and assessment of Gambella trade 1904–1935.* The International Journal of African Historical Studies, 20 (1), 75–94.

Baxter, P.T.W., & Hogg, R. (1990). *Property, poverty and people: changing rights in property and problems of pastoral development.* Manchester: University of Manchester Press.

Coronil, F (2001). Towards a Critique of Globalcentrism: Speculations on Capitalism's Nature. In Comarotte, J. and Comoroffuke, J. L. (Eds.). *Millennial Capitalism and the Culture of Neoliberalism,* 63-87. Durham and London: University Press.

Cotula, L. (2011). *Land Deals in Africa: What is in the Contracts?* London: IIED.

Cotula, L. (2012). The international political economy of the global land rush: A critical appraisal of trends, scale, geography and drivers. *Journal of Peasant Studies,* 39(3&4).

CSA Census (2007). *Population and Housing Census Report.* Central Statistical Agency (CSA). Addis Ababa: Federal Democratic Republic of Ethiopia.

Dereje, F. (undated). *Taking the Bull by Its Horns: Expanding the Natural Resource Base and Tackling the Root Causes of Conflict.* Pax Christi, the Netherlands.

Dereje, F. (2006). *Differing Identity Discourses, Differing Ethnicities: Comparing the Anywaa and the Nuer.* Berlin: Max Planck Institute for Social Anthropology.

Dereje, F. (2007). *The Interface between National and Regional Level Decisions and Local Conflicts in the Gambella Region.* Research Report submitted to Pact in support of Pact Ethiopia's Restoration of Community Stability in Gambella Project and Constructive Dialogue Initiative Project.

Dereje, F. (2009). *The Current Conflict Situation in the Gambella Region and Suggestions for Sustainable Peace-building, With a Special Reference to the Baro River.* Research Report submitted to Pact, Ethiopia.

De Schutter, O. (2011). How not to think of land-grabbing: three critiques of large-scale investments in farmland. *The Journal of Peasant Studies*, 38 (2), 249–279.

Dessalegn, R. (2008). *The peasant and the state: Studies in Agrarian change in Ethiopia 1950-2000s*. Addis Ababa: AAU Press.

Devereux, S. (2007). Cashing in or crashing out? Pastoralist livelihoods in Somali Region, Ethiopia. Institute of Development Studies, University of Sussex, Prepared for the Living on the Margins Conference, Stellenbosch 26–28 March, 2007.

Devereux, S. (2010). Better Marginalised than Incorporated? Pastoralist Livelihoods in Somali Region, Ethiopia. *European Journal of Development Research*, 22(5), 678–695.

Duany, W. (1992). *Neither places nor prison: the constitution of order among the Nuer*. PhD thesis. Program of the Department of Political Science and School of Public and Environmental Affairs, Indiana University.

FDRE (1993). *Constitution*. Addis Ababa: Federal Democratic Republic of Ethiopia (FDRE).

Flintan, F. (2011). *Broken lands. Broken lives? Causes and impacts of land fragmentation in the rangelands of Ethiopia, Kenya and Uganda*. Report for REGLAP, Nairobi.

Fouad, M. (2012). Power and property: commercialization, enclosures, and the transformation of agrarian relations in Ethiopia. *Journal of Peasant Studies*, 39(1), 81–104.

Gerike, C. (n.d.). *Reading the land: An introduction to cultural landscape*. Anthropological Studies Center, Sonoma State University.

Gambella Regional State (2010). *Villagization Programme Implementation Manual 2010*. Addis Abeba.

Getachew, G., Solomon, D., & Coppock, D. L. (Eds.) (2004). *Pastoralism in Ethiopia and the Policy Environment: Linking Research, Development Actors, and Decision-Makers*. Summary of proceedings for a meeting held 15 August 2003 at the International Livestock Research Institute (ILRI), Addis Ababa, Ethiopia.

GTP I (2010). *First Growth and Transformation Plan (GTP I)*, Ministry of Finance and Economic Development (MOFED). Addis Ababa: Federal Democratic Republic of Ethiopia.

Hagmann, T., & Speranza, I. (2010). New Avenues for Pastoral Development in sub-Saharan Africa. *European Journal of Development Research*, 22, 593–604.

Hall, R. (2011). *Land Grabbing in Africa and the New Politics of Food*, Policy Brief-041. Future Agricultures Consortium.

Harvey, D. (2003). *The New Imperialism*. Oxford: Oxford University Press.

Hatfield and Davies (2006). *Global Review of the Economics of Pastoralism*. Prepared for the World Initiative for Sustainable Pastoralism. IUCN, Nairobi.

Helland, J. (2006). *Land Tenure in the Pastoral Areas of Ethiopia*. Paper presented at the International Research Workshop on Property Rights, Collective Action and Poverty Reduction in Pastoral Areas of Afar and Somali National Regional State, Ethiopia, 30–31 October.

HRW (2011). *World Report*. New York: Human Rights Watch (HRW).

Keeley et al (2014). James Keeley, Wondwosen Michago Seide, Abdurehman Eid and Admasu Lokaley Kidewa. *Large-scale land deals in Ethiopia: Scale, trends, features and outcomes to date*. London: IDRC and IIED.

Lavers, T. (2011). *The role of foreign investment in Ethiopia's smallholder-focused agricultural development strategy*. Paper presented at the International Conference on Global Land Grabbing, 6–8 April, organised by the Land Deals Politics Initiative (LDPI) and *Journal of Peasant Studies* and hosted by the Future Agricultures Consortium. Institute of Development, Studies, University of Sussex.

Little, P.D., McPeak, J., Barrett, C.B., & Kristjanson, P. (2008). Challenging Orthodoxies: Understanding Poverty in Pastoral Areas of East Africa. *Development and Change*, 587–611.

Little, P.D., Behnke, R., McPeak, J., & Getachew, G. (2010a). *Retrospective Assessment of Pastoral Policies in Ethiopia, 1991-2008, Report Number 1, Pastoral Economic Growth and Development Policy Assessment, Ethiopia*. Commissioned by the UK Government's Department for International Development (DfID) at the request of the Government of Ethiopia.

Little, P.D., McPeak, J., Getachew, G., & Behnke, R. (2010b). *5 Future Scenarios for Pastoral Development in Ethiopia, 2010-2025, Report Number 2, Pastoral Economic Growth and Development Policy Assessment, Ethiopia*.

Makki, F (2012). Power and property: commercialization, enclosures, and the transformation of agrarian relations in Ethiopia. *Journal of Peasant Studies, 39*:1, 81–104.

McDowell, C., & de Haan, A. (1997). *Migration and Sustainable Livelihoods: A Critical Review of the Litrature*. IDS Working Paper 65. Institute of Development, Studies, University of Sussex.

Meyer, S. (2007). *Susan Sontag's 'Archaeology of Longings'*, Texas Studies in Literature and Language, 49, 1, 45-63.

MoA (2013), Public Relations Bureau Press Release, 18 September 2013.

MOARD (2009). *The 2009 Agricultural Potential Report of Ethiopia*. Ministry of Agriculture and Rural Development (MOARD). Addis Ababa: Federal Democratic Republic of Ethiopia.

Moritz, M. (2008). Competing Paradigms in Pastoral Development? A Perspective from the Far North of Cameroon. *World Development*, 36(11), 2243–2254.

Mosely, J. (2012). *Peace, Bread and Land: Agricultural Investments in Ethiopia and the Sudans*. Briefing Paper AFP BP 2012/01, Chatham House, London.

Medhane, T. (2007). *Gambella: The Impact of Local Conflict on Regional Security*. Institute of Security Studies (ISS), Pretoria, and Center for Policy Research and Dialogue (CPRD), Addis Ababa.

Mahmoud, A. (2004). *Pastoral Development Strategies and Policies in Ethiopia: A Critical Analysis and Evaluation*. Proceedings of the Third National Conference, Pastoralist Forum in Ethiopia. Addis Ababa: Pastoralist Forum in Ethiopia.

Mousseau, F and Sosnoff, G. (2011). *Understanding Land Investment Deals in Africa. Country Report: Ethiopia*. Oakland Institute, Oakland, USA.

Mussa, M. (2004). *A comparative study of pastoralist parliamentary group: Case study on the pastoral affairs standing committee of Ethiopia*. Natural Resources Institute (NRI) and the Pastoral and Environmental Network in the Horn of Africa (PENHA).

Narula, S., Liu, W., Mittal, A., Mousseau, F., Sinha, G. A., Stern, R. (2013) *Unheared Voices: The Human Rights Impact of Land Investments on Indigenous Communities in Gambella*. Briefing Paper, Oakland Institute, Oakland, USA.

Rahmeto, D. (2009). *The peasant and the State, studies in agrarian change in Ethiopia 1950s-2000s*. Addis Ababa University Press.

Rettberg, S. (2010). Contested narratives of pastoral vulnerability and risk in Ethiopia's Afar region. *Pastoralism*, 1(2), 248–273.

Sommer, M. (2005). *Transforming Conflict in the multi-ethnic State of Gambella in Ethiopia: Mediation in a divided society*. Institut Universitaire Kurt Böschs.

Taylor, K. (2008). *Landscape and Memory: cultural landscapes, intangible values and some thoughts on Asia*. In 16th ICOMOS General Assembly and International Symposium: 'Finding the spirit of place – between the tangible and the intangible', 29 September–4 October 2008, Quebec, Canada

Tesfa-Alem, T. (2013). *Ethiopia to Build Road Linking It With Sudan, South Sudan, Kenya*. Sudan Tribune, 2013-03-08.

Turner, M.D. (2009). Capital on the move: The changing relation between livestock and labor in Mali, West Africa. *GeoForum*, 40(5), 746–755.

Van der Post, L. (1987). *A Walk with a White Bushman*, London: Penguin.

White B., Borras, Jr, S. Hall, R., Scoones, I. & Wolford, W. (2012). The new enclosure: Critical perspectives corporate land deals. *The Journal of Peasant Studies*, 39(30-4), 619–647.

Yohannes, G., Magagi, S., Bayer, W. & Waters-Bayer, A. (2011). *More than climate change: pressures leading to innovation by pastoralists in Ethiopia and Niger*. Paper presented at the international conferences on the Future of Pastoralism, 21–23 March, organized by Future Agriculture Consortium, University of Sussex and the Feinstein International Center, Tufts University.

Index

Current African Issues (CAI)

Current African Issues (CAI) is a book series published by the Nordic Africa Institute since 1981. As the title implies, it raises and analyses current and topical issues concerning Africa. All CAI books are academic works by researchers in the social and multidisciplinary sciences.

Previous titles in the CAI series:

63 *Agricultural water institutions in East Africa*; Atakilte BEYENE (ed); 2015

62 *Dammed divinities : the water powers at Bujagali Falls, Uganda*; Terje OESTIGAARD; 2015

61 *African conflicts, development and regional organisations in the post-Cold War international system*; Victor A. O. ADETULA; 2015

60 *The role of food banks in food security in Uganda : the case of the Hunger Project food bank, Mbale epicentre*; Joseph WATULEKE; 2015

59 *Resettled for development : the case of New Halfa agricultural scheme, Sudan*; Marianna WALLIN; 2014

58 *Youth and the labour market in Liberia : on history, state structures and spheres of informalities*; Emy LINDBERG; 2014

57 *Current status of agriculture and future challenges in Sudan*; Farida MAHGOUB; 2014

56 *Election-related violence : the case of Ghana*; Clementina AMANKWAAH; 2013

55 *Academics on the move : mobility and institutional change in the Swedish development support to research capacity building in Mozambique*; Måns FELLESSON and Paula MÄHLCK; 2013

54 *The oil industry in Uganda : a blessing in disguise or an all too familiar curse?*; Pamela K. MBABAZI; 2013

53 *Sweden-Norway at the Berlin conference 1884-85 : history, national identity-making and Sweden's relations with Africa*; David NILSSON; 2013

52 *Musical violence : gangsta rap and politics in Sierra Leone*; Boima TUCKER; 2013

51 *Favouring a demonised plant : Khat and Ethiopian smallholder enterprise*; Gessesse DESSIE; 2013

50 *From global land grabbing for biofuels to acquisitions of African water for commercial agriculture*; David Ross OLANYA; 2012

49 *Water scarcity and food security along the Nile : politics, population increase and climate change*; Terje OESTIGAARD; 2012

48 *Transnational activism networks and gendered gatekeeping : negotiating gender in an African association of informal workers*; Ilda LINDELL; 2011

47 *Natural resource governance and EITI implementation in Nigeria*; Musa ABUTUDU and Dauda GARUBA; 2011

46 *African migration, global inequalities, and human rights : connecting the dots*; William MINTER; 2011

45 *The agrarian question in Tanzania? : a state of the art paper*; Razack B. LOKINA, Sam MAGHIMBI and Mathew A. SENGA; 2011

44 Understanding poverty in Africa? : a navigation through disputed concepts, data and terrains; Mats HÅRSMAR; 2010

43 China, India, Russia and the United States : the scramble for African oil and the militarization of the continent; Daniel VOLMAN; 2009

42 *Persuasive preventio : towards a principle for implementing Article 4(h) and R2P by the African Union*; Dan KUWALI; 2009

41 *Africa's development in the 21st century : reshaping the research agenda*; Fantu CHERU; 2008

40 *The African economy and its role in the world economy*; Arne BIGSTEN and Dick DUREVALL; 2008

39 *Natural resources in sub-Saharan Africa : assets and vulnerabilities*; Johan HOLMBERG; 2008

38 *Demography and the development potential of sub-Saharan Africa*; Bo MALMBERG; 2008

37 *Migration in sub-Saharan Africa*; Aderanti ADEPOJU; 2008

OPEN ACCESS

You can find these, and earlier titles in the CAI series, in our digital archive Diva, www.diva-portal.org, where they are also available as open access resources for any user to read or download at no cost.

www.ingramcontent.com/pod-product-compliance
Lightning Source LLC
Chambersburg PA
CBHW060829270326
41931CB00003B/106